Poetic Memories of Harlem U.S.A

James B. Cohen, Sr.

iUniverse, Inc.
Bloomington

Poetic Memories of Harlem U.S.A

iUniverse books may be ordered through booksellers or by contacting:

iUniverse
1663 Liberty Drive
Bloomington, IN 47403
www.iuniverse.com
1-800-Authors (1-800-288-4677)

Because of the dynamic nature of the Internet, any web addresses or links contained in this book may have changed since publication and may no longer be valid. The views expressed in this work are solely those of the author and do not necessarily reflect the views of the publisher, and the publisher hereby disclaims any responsibility for them.

Any people depicted in stock imagery provided by Thinkstock are models, and such images are being used for illustrative purposes only.

Paula Bonner, Editor and PR.
Angela R.Cohen, Photographer

Certain stock imagery © Thinkstock.

ISBN: 978-1-4502-9954-1 (sc)
ISBN: 978-1-4502-9955-8 (ebk)

Printed in the United States of America

iUniverse rev. date: 08/15/2011

Poetic Memories of Harlem U.S.A

∾ <u>Pauline's Birthday</u> ∾

My beloved wife in July had a birthday
Celebration
You should have seen her mother
perform this afro - centric dance
It's a dance the ancestors do when they
see their child advance
Rest assured they'll be a party to
commemorate this day
And though you will not see them
they'll be there anyway
So as we all salute you on this most
important day
We pray that God's love and blessings
be with you in every way

Dedicated to the memory of my beloved wife
Pauline Mathews Cohen
1934—2005

Table of Contents

Hip Hop

Harlem was alive in the 60s
The future looked bright for the 70s
The missing pieces were in place
The scars of the past might be erased
The cracks in the wall could be plastered
Our dependency on welfare might be mastered
Unlimited optimism was not just a dream
The masses knew all things were possible if
the slate were clean
Perhaps you can hear the drums of the day
And see the twilight that ended the fray
Of course we were happy as a new born tot
America promised a chicken for every pot
So politically we hip hopped down the road
Never knowing if the next amendment from
Congress
soon might explode

The Mecca

Harlem was the original Mecca for black life in
America
The world beat a path to her door to join in
the hysteria
The Apollo, Cotton Club and Savoy
ballroom led the grand parade
Events at these clubs lasted longer
than a decade
In the midst of this excitement the
Renaissance of Black literature
emerged
Langston Hughes and James Baldwin
navigated this literary surge
Duke Ellington, Count Basie and Lena Horne
through music received world wide
acclaim
Thus these legends and events made the
Mecca known as Harlem live up to its
name

Apollo Theatre

Black Harlems gift to the world was the famous
Apollo theatre
No public venue provided music that was greater
World famous artist filled the patrons heart with
tons
of music glee
The natives sang, danced and supported the
Apollo faithfully
After a matinee movie ended, the curtain on the
stage was raised
The expectations of the patrons left them in a daze
You did not see the band but you heard this soulful
beat
Immediately thereafter the only sound you heard
was
that of tapping feet
The musicians with their marcels indeed were very
dapper,
the chorus girls were pretty and comedians were
as
glib as any modern rapper
The Apollo was not a movie house, it was an
institution
Its halls contain more legends than in our
constitution

Gypsies

In the autumn of each year, October to
be precise
Hundreds of Euro-nomadic gypsies found
Harlem rather nice
They leased all vacant stores from one end to
the other
Eighth Ave due to length was their choice
above all others
Gypsies loved the color red and fabrics made of
velvet
They loved to read a patrons palm and if you did
not
see the ace of spades, no reason for alarm
Beyond a doubt the gypsy lifestyle was filled with
mystic charm
At the 3 to 4 week mark on orders from their
leader they always journeyed on

I looked for many years but they never did return
fore when those drugs reached Harlem it was
grounds for grave concern

The Boogeyman

In Harlem he was known as the
boogeyman
He scared the children and they
always ran
No one claims to have ever seen
him
Those who have said he's a
demon
He seems to come when you dim
the lights

He boogies best on given nights
But in those days he was rather
listless
He liked the kids and mommies
knew this
But times have changed and now
he's ruthless
Thus the word these days is watch
your back
Cause the boogeyman who once was
fictional now plays around with
crack

Tribute to Malcolm

Malcolm Shabazz said the chickens would
come home to roost
He told no lie because the brothers are on
the loose
They got themselves some oozies and there
taking no abuse
The problem that prevails is there filling up
The jails
Now Malcolm knew this would happen
since the children of the oppressed were no
longer laughing
He recognized the viciousness of the game
known as Jim Crow
It always blocked and stifled the black mans
right to grow
He pleaded with the powers to please unlock
the coop
They claimed there was no key; so if you
hear the sound of chickens then you know there
coming home to roost

Snow In The Hood

Harlem was so pretty when snow fell in the
hood
We loved the deep white snow as only children
could
The purity of the snow hid the meanness of the
streets

It covered all the hydrants and made the doggies
cheat
Now when the doggies cheated the snow was not
the same
Where it once was white as rice, it was no longer
nice
This quickly ended our quest for fun and games
since yellow mushy snowmen reduced our joy
to pain

Mary Juanna

There was this very pretty lady whose name
was Mary Juanna

Her name rhymed with a lethal drug known
as marijuana

Thus our Spanish was upgraded without even
going to school

As kids who knew not why we thought the word
was cool

The white sticks looked like cigarettes but the
scent mean't there'd be regrets

So kids who smoked joints in their teens
endeavored
to hide but were always seen

Cause the lady with the funny name wants to
know if
you will play her game

DO   YOU   WANNA

Ole Saint Nicholas

The parks in Harlem were very beautiful
Throughout the year they all were easily
accessible
St. Nicholas was the largest and by far
the prettiest
Thus when spring and summer rolled around
it was indeed the busiest
But deep within its beauty were many slippery
rocks
We played no foot or baseball since the park
was awfully hilly
Thus the only choice we had was to do things
rather silly
My childhood park still stands today although
its old and grey
But nonetheless its love for kids still calls for
them to come and play

<u>Marcus Garvey</u>

MARCUS GARVEY LIKE MOST BLACK LEADERS
WAS AT TIMES MISUNDERSTOOD

HE CHALLENGED THE DEPTHS OF BLACK
DESPAIR
AND GRIEVED WITH ALL WHO WOULD

THE RECORD SHOWS HIS BATTLE CRY WAS
"RISE YOU MIGHTY BLACK PEOPLE"

THESE WORDS ECHOED THROUGH THE LAND,
NO
OTHER PHRASE TOUCHED THIS DEMAND

NOW GARVEY HAD A MASTER PLAN TO
RETURN
FOLKS TO THE MOTHERLAND

IT WAS TO BE AN ACT OF LOVE BUT
BROTHERS
WENT AND TOLD THE MAN

GARVEYS DREAM OF "BACK TO AFRICA" did
indeed collapse

BUT GARVEYS LOVE FOR HIS PEOPLE NEVER
DID ELAPSE

The Night of the Riot

In the year of "48" on a hot, hot summers night
A rumor flashed through Harlem faster than the
speed of light
Some said a black soldier was shot down by a
cop

No degree of civil protest made the issue stop

The riot went from street to street

The looting and the fires created awesome heat

No white owned stores dodged the venom

The anger of the hood said to hell with them
let's get ''em".

In Memory of Congress Lady Shirley Chisholm

Shirley Chisholm was the first black congress-
woman and her spirit was extraordinary
Despite the odds against her she was a
visionary
She challenged the concepts of her party to
run for President
She said that being black was no hindrance,
just a chance to set a precedence
She walked in Soujorner's and Harriet
Tubmans footsteps and bowed to no
ungodly man
Her tenacity for justice, made her take a
stand
She battled for her people in the corridors of
Congress
Thus the legacy she leaves us, is some may fight
for more
but none can fight for less

Numbers

Many folks pursued an awesome dream
They dreamed of sugar coated numbers that
promised a life of sweet ice cream
In reality it was a lottery where their pennies
and their dollars kept them in a game
Unfortunately if their runner failed to pay ,they
had no one to blame
Folks placed their heart and soul in the numbers
game
But gambling never paved the road to happiness
or fame
The hopes and dreams of all these folks was
undeniably real
They risked their hard earned money and hoped
for a better deal
The game of numbers never supported poor
peoples dreams
It only made them vulnerable to other man made
schemes

The Community

The questions often asked what's wrong with
our community

We like to laugh and play and yet we have no
unity
Some decades back our eyes focused on the
sparrow
Then we lost our backbone and our spine
grew weak and narrow
A small amount of prosperity made us suspect
towards each other
Once we compromised we could not
trust a brother
We're short on ownership of stores in our
community
Could it be a lack of capitol or some force
we cannot see
But if we put our best foot forward we control
our destiny
Since dollars and some common sense rule
this economy

The Ice Box

Before refrigeration most food left
over spoiled
Therefore you ate it all for there was
no second call
Now the ice box in those days held
a block of frozen ice
Thus the ice man grinned from ear to
ear if you had to call him twice
When winters fury came along you
placed food on a window sill
Mother nature as she always did provided
the timely chill
Once summer came old boxes no longer
useful soon were confiscated
Sad to say some kids found them as a
place to play and soon were
suffocated

Cold Water Flats

The cold water flat in Harlem was a wretched
place to live
When winter winds came calling it blew thru
like a sieve
Not having heat or hot water made matters
even worse
Thus those who dwelled within presumably
would curse
Now toilets for its occupants left much to be
desired
But poverty in the city mean't your personal
rights expired
And though these flats had no e-lec-tricity
the slumlord took his rent each month and
denied com-pli-city

A Clear Day

To know Harlem is to love her, she's

45 blocks in length from 110th-155th

On a clear day with 20-20 vision your

eyes will defy your imagination

She'll reveal a sight not far away and

subject your senses to a point

of stimulation

There can be no denial that this is a

revelation

Therefore at 155th a monster structure

confirms your observation

No village on the planet boasts such a

natural wonder but Harlem does,

let no man put asunder

Winoes

The wino of the 50s was relatively harmless

He took whatever you gave and sometimes even
less

Harlem took him for granted, since he was always
low
on luck

He worked, he smiled, he cried, until you gave a
buck

And though you knew he'd get no better the hood

shed no tears, not even a letter

They slept overnight in hallways and doorways

And drank so much booze, they glowed like a fuse

They started drinking when they were young,
presumably
just for fun

But when Satan provided that extra rum, there
was no
place for them to run

In line with their addiction, they were running out of time

And as the hood moved on, they sadly fell behind

The Speakeasy

Once upon a time it was known as the speakeasy
It was a place to socialize, although its clientele
was
sleazy
They drank a lot of liquor, home brewed, unhealthy
and illegal
However the poor souls that consumed it, cared
less that
it was lethal
The booze they drank had many names among
them
sneaky pete
Thus after short indulgence they quickly went to
sleep
And though speakeasies are of days long gone
To those who do remember its like a sad, sad
song

Strivers Row

In Harlem there is a street that's really quite
unique,
it's nickname focused on the lifestyle of those
who were elite
This elegant tree lined street of yellow brownstone
houses was also symbolic of those who financially
were discreet
Strivers Row was home to politicians, doctors,
artists
and other professionals
The standard for Strivers Row was hard work and
determination, the inhabitants left no room for
failure or even contemplation
Strivers Row has a secret that I and others know,
we'll gladly share it with you than
leave it in escrow
Today Strivers Row is a New York city landmark,
its glow at the end of the tunnel guides
strivers through the night

116 TH Street

The destination of the Columbia student was
the university
Before some ever reached it they faced   adversity
The route was clear yet mistakes were very
numerous
And once they boarded the "AA" their trip
was less than humorous

This blunder on the "AA" left them at 116th street
They are in the heart of the drug complex and
really are fresh meat
So as they flinch in agony and struggle to the
street the brothers are there to greet them it
looks just like a fleet
Now they lose all that they owned but did not
lose their life
Fore the frenzy of the brothers ire was as lethal
as their knife

The Backyard

The backyard of tenement houses was a
convenient place to play

It was unhealthy and quite hazardous in
almost every way
We played amidst the broken bottles,
garbage and tin cans
And once we dodged our neighbors dogs
we laughed and clapped our hands
A playground would have been the
answer but there was no park
near by
So as we played and hip hopped thru the
weeds our mommies were not happy
but it did not make them cry

Black Asphalt

As kids the paving of the streets in Harlem
was an exciting event to see
Big trucks poured the molten asphalt and
stout hearted men spread it easily
The men wore hip length boots to ward off
the searing heat
Fore if it touched your skin it would also
cook your meat
The scent from the heated asphalt was indeed
quite nauseating, especially if you stood to
close and found it captivating
The men appeared to be first generation
immigrants of Italian ancestry
This was not surprising since Italians in New
York controlled this industry
Black asphalt still paves our city streets but
machines not men deprive kids of this
old time treat

Up on the Roof

In Harlem we often played up on the roof
At times it got quite scary, no lie that is
the truth
The buildings were at least five stories
tall
And sad to say some kids I knew did fall
While leaping roof to roof one day I had my
greatest scare
I barely missed an open shaft and yes I said
a prayer
My childhood almost slipped away that day
Therefore I learned that roof tops were no
place to play

Something to Eat

Our meal most days was lima bean
It filled our empty bellies and then we
all would scream
And on a day when all went well we
even had some pork
We ate those fatty pig tails and did not
need a fork
Now when it came to lunch we loaded
up on spam
Boy that was some greasy meat cause
it came right out the can
With seven mouths to feed we never
had no beef
I see now that the cost of it would only
cause more grief

A Boyhood Friend

His name was Toach, no he was not a roach

Why such a nickname, I have no idea

We lived in Harlem as boy hood friends

Never drinking or smoking despite the trends

We laughed, played and rooted for the Giants

Long before the major leagues had any black
clients

While watching football in December, we often
grew quite cold

I guess we did not have much sense, that's why
we were so bold

Toach had two pretty sisters and an alcoholic dad

The girls were slightly frisky, and the musty boys
were glad

Now once we reached our teenage years, Toach
started getting
heavy
He then began to diet and even started drinking

He was not drinking cognac and so he started
sinking

I do remember Toach, for once upon a time he
was above
reproach

Martyr's For Peace

All Christians will acknowledge that Christ
died to pay the price
So what does it say for others who make the
sacrifice
Our eulogies for Malcolm, King and Garvey told
us of their strife
Thus the freedom that we have today was
fueled and spirited by their life
And as the life of Christ serves as a model to
us all
The cross these black men carried means they
also heard the call

In Memory of Emmett Till

Emmett Till was 14 years of age when he
visited Mississippi

He saw this skinny white girl and he
hollered yippee

He had a right to speak to anyone he liked

But that cracker in Mississippi said boy that
just ain't right

So two low life crackers dragged Emmett
off into the night

They took his mortal life at some rural
site

Now the murderers were caught and brought
before a jury

But a body of their red neck peers said their
actions showed no fury

So once again there was no justice

And the government after 50 years seeks
to once again placate us

The Jewish Grocer

As a youngster I worked for a Jewish
grocer
I delivered lots of groceries, our
clientele was black so none of
it was kosher
Many of our customers were short
until payday
However this Jewish grocer granted
credit on folks solemn vow to pay
This business and humanitarian gesture
helped a lot of folks move forward
Thus black folks need to eat was
nurtured by this Jewish grocer

The Choir

Long before crack ever came along
The drug dealer played a different
song
The tune they played was heroin
The lyrics were strange but folks
joined in
Now you had to hold a certain note
Since heroin made you lie, steal and
float
And when the master devil called your
name you sniffed horse up your nose
or shoved in your vein
This was the melody long before crack
and each melodic note put you
flat on your back

The Brown Bomber

This nickname described a black man whose
talent
was extraordinarily special
His real name was Joseph Louis Barrow and his
gift
from God was as pure as a golden vessel
As a boxer he was not ordinary the explosiveness
in his left fist left his opponents listless
Joe was revered by Harlemites and on nights that
he fought not a creature was stirring not
even a mice
On nights that he fought Harlem came to a
standstill,
folks were glued to their radios and the streets
were bare
Upon Joe being victorious even the street lights
had
an unusual glare
Joe was as modest as he was humble and at
times
he even mumbled but inside the ring he did his
thing
Joe was a national treasure and for all who knew
and loved him it was indeed a
pleasure

Polo Grounds

This was the home stadium of the baseball team
New York Giants
It was located on the cutting edge of Harlem
at 155th Street
I remember being in attendance, the stadium
and the team were lily white
As a child of ten or eleven years I loved baseball
so presumably everything was right
The logistics of the stadium placed it near the
Harlem River thus the fans were blessed
with a gentle breeze
On alternate hot and sultry weekends the Negro
Leagues prevailed
Black baseball was superb and thought there were
some heated rivalries n one went to jail
The end of the Polo Grounds era was void of any
trauma
The residents of Harlem has issues that presented
greater drama

Mandela

South Africa sentenced Nelson Mandela to 27
years in jail

The system was so racist that it even denied
him bail
The world took notice of this act of inhumane
injustice
Thus protest all around the world created
quite a ruckus
South Africa refused to release Mandela
and vowed to not repent
But God was in control and South Africa
did relent
The measure of this man was he expressed
no bitterness
This quality defined the man Mandela and
reflected on his greatness

A Dilemma

The demise of our communities can be traced
to fragmentation

It coincided with a desire to pursue
integration

Our humility made us sensitive to the cries
of exploitation

We dropped our guard and in return
we suffered indignation

Ancestral pride would have avoided this
humiliation

But once we made the choice our morality
gave way to degradation

We should have run and cut our losses, to
prevent any further molestation

Now things have got so bad, that its time
for contemplation
So before we get down on our knees,
three cheers for reparation

It means that someone owes us something
from the days of the plantation

My Friend Reggie

Reggie and I met as boys on the street of dreams
Because of where we lived we played on different
teams
He came from uptown Harlem, endowed with lots
of
talent
His love for basketball was equivalent to a baby
and
its parent
On a warm summers night at the Harlem Boys
club
we envisioned our dreams in a college career
Ironically our goals were met in our freshman year
Our lives ran parallel long after
this fact
And the bond of friendship remained eternally
intact

How Could I Know

He hung around until my birthday
And passed away the next succeeding day
Three weeks ago he said he felt quite ill
And as the optimist, I said just take a pill
From 900 miles away how could I know
the bells had rung and the cock would crow
I stayed in touch until the end when an e-mail
told me of my friend
The church was packed and Harlem was cold
Closure took place as the scriptures foretold

(Feb. 1936—Nov. 2003)

Major League Baseball

As a kid growing up in Harlem I was an avid
baseball fan
But during those hateful years no one played
except the man
As graceful and as talented as the brothers
were back then the major leagues said "no" you
can't play with mister Charlie or Uncle Ben
Now I was a loyal Giant fan
I knew each white ballplayer by his tan
They ran and hit the ball quite well
But once Jackie, Hank and Willie came you knew
who rang the bell

Jews and the Black Community

The Jewish impact on Harlem was extraordinary

History may reveal that their presence was quite necessary

There impact in the community took second place to none

Its no wonder there zest for doing business came as

However benevolent acts revealed their spiritual heart

And where it's been confirmed they gave some blacks
their start

Now as the intellect and spirit of black folks rose

The Jewish impact in Harlem slowly came to a close

The Projects

I lived in Harlem when the projects came
Many people needed housing and were feeling
substantial pain
It was a blessing in disguise to see new buildings
rise
Apparently the politicians heard the peoples
soulful
cries
As the decades passed, some questions began
unfolding
Why were so many people living and dying in
these buildings
The idea as conceived was great as seen on
paper
But the reality was, the people were no safer

He Died for Us

He should have been protected
The nation now knows he was neglected
Dr. King feared not for his life
He knew his calling entailed strife
Dr. King made mankind rise and see the
light
He knew his fight for civil rights was
right
Dr. King was awarded the prestigious Nobel
Peace prize
But when he saw through the darkness, we
all had blindfolds on our
eyes

The First

What does being the oldest mean
Am I the leader of the team
I was the first of seven born
Maybe that's why Gabriel blew his horn
My momma sometimes served my dinner first
That made daddy mad and he would curse
As I grew older and sought advice
There were no wise old mentors, so I had to
pay the price
I had no older siblings and knew not what to do
So when it came to most things, I did not have
a clue
Thank god for the gift of common sense
For when I learned to use it, I was no longer tense

No Place To Hide

Vacant buildings created serious problems
for people in the hood
The emptiness of these dwellings obstructed
community efforts to do good
These buildings undermined the welfare of
the kids at play
Thus mommies stayed alert to monitor
those who prey
No doubt these dwellings were an eyesore
Only the sound of their demolition made
mommies smile and roar
If such dwellings were systematically aborted
perhaps the lives of many would not have
been distorted

Homelessness

In Harlem long ago they also were called
homeless
They slept and dined in hallways and needed
no address
They worked a little, drank a lot and had few
decent clothes
And though their lifestyle was peculiar,
they said its what they chose
They placed no blame upon society and ducked
the glare of notoriety
The hood had no axe to grind with them
They weren't criminals, only homeless men

The City Game

Spaldeen was the name printed on the ball
This brand was best whenever you played
stick ball
In Harlem the street beneath your feet gave
you squatters rights to compete
You had to have a mop stick, broom stick or
whatever
If the length was right, the ball flew like
a feather
The measurement of our playing field went
sewer hole to sewer hole
So if you got a two base hit, you understood
your role
Quite often you could hear a window break
if the ball you hit did not go straight
When police arrived on the scene they always
took our mop sticks, broom sticks and
spaldeens

The Mascot

Once upon a time stickball was big in Harlem
The big boys chose me as a mascot and
resolved a minor problem
My team was known as the Eagles of 132nd street
Thus being selected as their mascot made
me feel unique
I was 14 years of age, they were 16 up to 22
so it was indeed apparent they had me by a few
My duty as a mascot was to go to a buildings roof
I retrieved all loose spaldeens, dodged some
vicious
dogs and when they failed to catch me I turned
and hollered woof
Now jumping roof to roof really was insane
But visualize my joy when my Eagles won the
game

The Attempt

As we struggle for our lawful and god given
right
We need a lot more muscle or we won't rest
well at night
Were losing in the streets and at the ballot box
If we don't turn it around we'll bow down to the
fox
We're constantly being outnumbered by voters
on the right
And because were on the left does not mean that
we cannot fight
But if we join with others who have a worthwhile
struggle we might find greater numbers
that we can use to juggle
And if one hand does not wash the other we've
lost nothing but a chance to help some
mother and a brother

How Long, Not Long

Were months from a presidential election year
So in Harlem what do we hear
The drums tell us civil rights is near
So what in the world do we have to fear
The scams may be like decades past
Make no mistake the dyes been cast
The politicians always loved us
But who among them gave us justice
Our lot has been the okey- doke
Well, just which generation ends the joke
Garvey, Malcolm, King and Vesey tried their best
to break the mold
But cell phones, A,K,A, materialism replaced the
void within our soul

A Childs Rememberance of Wartime

I was but a child when world war 2
was over
Mankind was overjoyed that the threat
to peace was lower
No more would wailing sirens scare me
in the night
No more would burly M.P.s arrest A.W.O.L.
soldiers who did not want to fight
No more would nighttime blackouts deprive
me of the light
Now the light will shine and keep me free
from fright
So as the world relaxed from an imminent danger
we began to laugh and play since war was now
a stranger

The Bigot

After all those bastard years he utters
that he's so ashamed
That as a U.S. Senator he played the
Jim Crow game
So as his day of judgment nears,
he pleads for mercy from his peers
But as a member of the Klan
he disrespected every man
So now he seeks to save his soul
amidst the rubble of the lives
he stole
He had no conscious when he bowed
down to the devil
And now he seeks to stand with men
of goodwill on the level

Between the Lines

You may recall when you were
but a child
The teacher said "stay within the
lines or put it on this pile
Now that you are older the rules
are still the same
You have to follow rules or you cannot
play the game
Some folks say they play by no one's
rules
Well what is a plumber who comes
without his tools
A drivers license, traffic light all have
regulations
So if you fail to make the rules
you have no reservation
That's just the way it is in this society
You stay within the lines or you
gain some notoriety

The Promise

A black man in 2008 is the nominee for U. S.
President
The constitution promised that one day
there'd be a precedent
The dream of all Americans is to have
their siblings qualify
They pray that with gods blessing their
siblings will survive to testify
What an honor it is to rise and be what
you choose to be
The journey won't be easy but if
you pay your dues
America promises her best to see
that you don't lose

Sailors in the City

As kids we sailed our boats downstream,
Many times before the streets were clean
city water trucks supplied the stream
Therefore when water flowed we all would scream
Old bottle caps and short match sticks were
ours to navigate
And once we donned our sailor caps indeed
our joy did escalate
We always stayed up on the curb never in
the street
And when our mommies saw us, they yelled
" boy wash your hands and come on home
to eat"

America

America is approaching the pinnacle
of her glorious existence
The founding fathers knew that if
we kept the faith one day
there'd be deliverance
So as 2008 unfolds we bear witness
to a panorama
Fore there's a black man on the
horizon whose name is
Barack Obama
Yes ,our forefathers and our ancestors
were limited in their vision
But deep in their hearts they knew,
some generation reaches this
decision
So as America moves towards its
date with destiny
The election of a woman or a black
man affirms her pledge to
dignity

Who Knows

I worked for the city back in the day
Like your j-o-b today, you toed the line
or you were sent away
Civil right groups suspected that test
we took were undermined
Thus research and commitment confirmed
they were not color blind
The basic fear was too many would excel
The plug was pulled and many brothers
fell
Thus the dreams of many were denied
Cause the system with no conscience, took them
for a ride

2004 Presidential Primary

Whether it was Kerry, Dean or Edwards
Al Sharpton was ignored
Despite what Sharpton had to say the voters
remained bored
He touched on all the issues and pledged to
honor voters wishes
Like Jackson in 88, they even wanted dishes
Traditionally black candidates always have a
problem
Most voters won't vote black and others remain
solemn
But Malcolm always said America will someday
pay
For voters who turn their backs and ignore
the ground rules of fair play

Polls

They took a poll the other day
It asked how white and black folks
spend their pay
So why this concern about our money
They stole the beehive, now they want
the honey
Our unemployment is at least ten percent
In many cases, we cant pay the
rent
SO they continue to worry about our income
Well that's very nice, maybe they might raise
it some
Now we know about such polls they never
focus on our goals
Yes, we could do a lot more with our
money
If you know who, was not so crummy

A Mothers Love

Yes, he was some mothers child
Behold the day that he was born and the
beauty of her smile
Her expectations for his future exceeded
the pain of the surgeons suture
She cried and prayed for his survival
But misdeeds in his life, left room for
no denial
So as he perches on a crane high up in the
midnight sky
His life a shambles and his mother cries;
I loved you son;
Why oh Why

No One Knows Like I Know

I shed many tears upon the death of my
beloved mama
If you've never had the experience then you
cannot know the trauma
Now as the years roll on my hearts found
some relief
But life being what it is you never lose the
grief
Thus one's capacity to weep must ultimately
be shared
Because the agonies of life leave none that
will be spared
So again my heart is systematically
attacked

Thus the creators message to us all is leave
your bags unpacked

U.S. President William Clinton

He was fair in the slicing of the pie
Right wingers, red necks and yes even
some blacks poked him in the eye
President Clinton made some mistakes
as all gods children do
He kept us out of war, uplifted the
economy and knew when he was
through
Thank god he had the heart to give
poor folks a break
And though he may have been
promiscuous he definitely
was no flake
Now the devil liked to call him
the black mans President
But it was his great humanity
that set a precedent

The Umbilical Journey

We fought for our freedom and
we gained it
But the umbilical cord was cut to soon
This linked us to our ancestors
and a foreseeable reward
Thus the road to glory would be
more than just another story
But as the road to victory drew near
our dependence on the cord grew
sheer
It was the virtues of the cord which
nurtured our dignity
Thus it is the basic tenet in life that
controls our destiny
So like a baby in its mothers womb
the cord of life cannot be cut
to soon

Freedom

A few decades ago, in the 60's to be exact
The system dissed us badly and made black folks
react
From Angela to Stokely the leadership was mad
The dignity of black folks had been questioned
and it
made most of us sad
Now the focus of the movement was to shed light
on
our strife
America had long ignored the merits of our gripe
So as we assembled on the streets to make our
voices
heard
We knew that God was on our side and judged us
by
our word

The Narrow Plank

For many immoral reasons our ancestors walked
the plank
They had no voice so pleas for mercy drew a
blank
Now the far end of the plank fed them to deep
sea fishes
And like the days of slavery no one heard their
wishes
But mans inhumanity will create more and
shorter planks
Thus future generations must work harder to
receive ancestral thanks

Kinetic Energy

As long as the sun is shining, ain't nothing gonna
turn me around

I have weathered the mighty storms and know
just what I have found

I sought the boundless energy that the mighty
sun provides

Thus my soul is lifted higher than that of the
rising tides

So if my lease on life becomes even more
profound

Then this I know for sure, ain't nothing gonna
turn me around

Soul Man

My soul doth cry and thru my eyes I weep

It happened when my momma died and Eddie
went to sleep

I remember Dr. King's last message to the world

He said his time had come and that his work was
done

Again my soul doth cries aloud and thru my eyes
I weep
For only months ago a dear friend found
eternal sleep
So as my soul weeps once again
Life must go on, despite the pain

Peanut Butter

As a child I grew up eating peanut butter
You could not talk while eating because it
made you stutter
The thickness of the substance at times
Stuck to your pallet
But if you rolled your tongue you did not
need a mallet
If you had a glass of milk it helped in
your digestion
But if you added jelly there were no
grounds for any question
So anytime your stomach growls like an air-
plane rudder get a slice of bread and
some skippy peanut butter

The Devil

I looked into the eyes of the devil and found
the playing field not level
He took prayer out of public schools
and left most teachers with one less tool
He scrapped the nations need for a
Pledge of Allegiance
Loyalty was replaced by mortal ignorance
There's a twinkle in his eye each time he
makes you cry
It's said he's a figment of our imagination
but his greatest joy comes with our humiliation
He's responsible for corruption, violence
and crack
And his best is yet to come if you don't
watch your back

Confusion

Can you remember as a kid, a day
you were uncomfortable
I remember such a day and found
it unexplainable
This church had a recreation center
It offered fun and games and no fee
to enter
Since it was a church the clergy were
all called father
I found this rather strange since my
father was at home
So who were these earthly men stealing
my daddies throne
As I hip hopped down the road of life
I found this in the bible twice
The scriptures stated what was logical
Call no earthly man your father if he is
not biological

Mother Katrina

A monster storm struck New Orleans

The fierceness of its roar muffled all
attempts to scream

Some politicians knew this awful day
would come

Thus torrent winds and raging waters
snuffed out lives and left no dreams
for some

This devastation of so many lives

Broke my heart as tears flowed
from my eyes

The Red Lobster

I have never eaten lobster and don't know if I
would

But many people like them, so apparently they
taste good

They are always in a tank, crawling on each other

The fact that they can crawl out, means you need
a cover

Well on a dark gray day while the lobsters were at
play

A thief came to this store, you knew he would not
pay

He reached into the tank, and grabbed a red, red
lobster

Who knows what made him stoop to this

Perhaps the taste of lobster is eternal bliss

Casanova

He was the janitor of a building on my block
His thick Jamaican accent solid as a rock
His passion for the game of baseball went from
spring to fall
Casanova's duties often were neglected until
he heard you call
But if he were debating baseball you got
no response at all
Now Casanova was his name, but historically
he had no legendary fame
Fore Casanova was a janitor, not a lover
and baseball was his game

Kudzu

Its a vine that grows a foot each night
So close your window and turn off the
lights
It came to Georgia from Japan
But the way it grew was not in the
plan
Georgia believed it would stop soil
erosion
Instead its abnormal growth created
great confusion
It covers houses, clings to poles and
kills most any tree
Attempts to kill it is an exercise in
futility
Georgia has been told this vine is
catastrophic
So if you stumble into some don't
become lethargic
Now the question still remains what
is this vine known as kudzu
Some say it can be eaten, I wouldn't
how about you?

China

On CNN the other day I saw the minister of
Bejin China speak

He spoke of China's will to work with others
towards world peace

Now China's glorious history has long been
documented

Thus the Minister proclaims China's role will
never be fragmented

Despite differences between China and the west

History has shown that men of goodwill
always rise and meet the test

Iraq

The western world is troubled by a place
known as Iraq
Its history of violence, a documented
fact

Their former despot leader, removed
and executed
Now the country must regroup before
its prostituted
The U.N. and the world have a monumental
task
Ancient sectarian issues can equate to
an empty flask
The world is optimistic that the different
sides can meet
But statesmen must explore all avenues
that lead the world to peace

The Solution

It was not Sadaam and it was not the oil

So why are we stuck on foreign soil

We hear such words as globalization,
protestation and molestation
But what really is the situation

Iraq's no stranger to internal strife

Since we've intervened we need to get it
right

It's a country like all others with so much to
gain

But it would be catastrophic to live or die
in vain

Terms of Enfearment

We lost the war on drugs
Now illegal immigration takes the stage
So what is more important: closing down
the borders or raising the minimum wage
Who knows when we will leave Iraq
The best minds say the decks been stacked
The issues grow much larger each and every
day
So where we've lost our peace of mind
perhaps we need to pray

The Creator

God made us in his image
The least of us is in his vintage
God foresaw the weakness in us all
when Adam and Eve failed to answer his call
God was aware his children needed guidance
They had an issue between love and violence
Thus the creator sent forth the 10 commandments
Gods children now possessed the sacred
sacraments
Now long before the flood, Noah was gods favorite
God gave the order for the Ark and Noah said I'll
build it
Gods cleansing of a sinful world took 40 days and
40 nights
What a pity it would be if he has to do it
twice

The Book of Life

We're familiar with books on medicine
and technology
The knowledge contained within even
includes historical mythology
But there is a book with greater credibility
Its written not with mortal hands therefore
there is no visibility
The author is almighty God who blesses
all with a stroke of his pen
Just imagine when those dark days come he's
there when you need a friend
He dots the "I" crosses the "T" and for his love
there is no fee
And when your days on earth are done he even
pens your legacy

"this is the book of life"

Dead Beat Daddies

Where have all the daddies gone
The kids are crying, please come home
Little boys now find their all alone
Their image maker just ain't home
Now mommies do the best they can
Love and kisses won't make a man
So if dead beat dads are a dilemma
Expect more boys to be called Emma

A New Car

THE MAN SAID YOU NEED NO JOB, CASH
OR CREDIT
WE HAVE THE CAR YOU WANT JUST COME
ON DOWN AND GET IT
NOW WANTING WHAT WAS OFFERED WITHOUT
A THOUGHT IN MIND
HE HIP HOPPED TO THE DEALERSHIP AND
HOLLERED "THIS IS MINE".
NOW THE DEALER SAID HOLD ON "JUST YOU
WAIT A MINUTE"
IF I CAN'T GET A POUND OF FLESH THEN YOU
MUST PAY THE LIMIT
SO HE WALKS AWAY FRUSTRATED AND
NEGLECTED
HE NOW KNOWS LACK OF COMMON SENSE
IS WHY HE WAS REJECTED

Car Thieves

Many years ago in the wild ,wild west
if you stole a cowboys horse they
hung you with the rest
Now days we have no horses but we
have some fancy cars
So if my SUV is stolen do we send the
thief to Mars
Now the crime does not equate with the act of
homicide
But I just wanna know who pays me for my ride
I cannot get to work and I owe the finance
company
If things don't get no better I just might lose my
honey
So if a car or horse thief steals your only ride
just remember those lovely rims that gave you
so much pride

Birds and Airplanes

A plane was spiraling in the Atlanta sky
I did not see it so I don't know why

Some say the noise was very frightening

Some rain was falling but really there
was no lightning
Just beyond the raindrops a small engine
plane was seen

Its peculiar errant spiral not on the radar
screen

Now its plunging towards the city, God
bless those in close proximity

An explosion occurs and some people die

Again were reminded only birds of a
feather unimpeded can fly

The Big Bailout

Were in the midst of a condition known as the big
bailout

Like a summer where you need some rain but
your
in a serious drought

Unscrupulous business practices have America in
a bind

Now short sighted politicians seek a formula to
bring us
from behind
Americans received a package designed to make
them happy
But bills that can't be paid just won't make
you sassy

America is borrowing from anyone and everyone

China loves us madly I wonder what we've done

Such outrageous conduct has America in a crisis

Therefore this bailout process better work or we'll
see
even higher prices

Cuba

Fidel Castro spoke on c-span just the
other day
It was his state of the union address
delivered every May
He proudly reported that Cuba's flag
still proudly flies
Despite the years of a U.S. blockade
and outrageous lies
With no financial support from the
World Trade Bank
Cuba's adversaries were sure they
would walk the plank
The countries education and economics
prevailed
Thus all efforts to topple this 3rd world
country failed

Michael

Michael Jackson was an extraordinary talent
Michaels sudden departure traumatized
the world for one eternal
moment
But the quality of his work will always
remain solvent
Michaels commitment to his fans explains
the world wide reverence found in
many lands
Michaels musical genius created lots of
happiness
But as we mourn his untimely death
it leaves us with an emptiness
Michaels genius may never be defined
but by the grace of God it will
stand the test of time
Michaels legacy to the world might well
be; 'MOURN NOT FOR MY LIFE"
I was sent by GOD to musically
share in your tribulations and your strife

Haiti

My soul cries out and thru my eyes
I weep
An earthquake struck the isle of Haiti
men, women and children
found eternal sleep
Earthquakes of this dimension bring
separation, desperation and
devastation
Thus thousands who had a future
died because of one bad
situation
Haitians know the word oppression,
can this tragedy bring forth
a resurrection
God knows Haiti will overcome
this threat to her
existence
Like many third world countries she
needs only humane assistance

Sugar Ray Robinson

Sugar Ray during his era was the best
in the game
Sugars good looks, skill and charisma
brought him fortune and fame
In the art of pugilism he was a master
among his peers
Thus his record of achievement will
endure for many years
The swiftness of his hands and feet
evaded the agony of
defeat
In Harlem he was equally as sweet,
he once owned many business's
on a certain street
Sugar will forever be an icon in the
sport of boxing
His skill and speed was sweeter than
any known toxin

Liberals vs. Conservatives

Our community has a problem with people
on the right
For some unknown reason they seem to want
to fight
We oppose each other politically and sometimes
philosophically
And when it comes to civil rights we must act
diplomatically
There must be some point in between that both
sides can agree
That if we meet each other halfway we can talk
civil—ly
Between a liberal and conservative this could
be the key
It's the most amicable way to resolve our
differences satisfactorily
Now we'll have on going problems with people
on the right
So we'll keep our eyes open, morning,
noon and night

U.S. President Barack Obama

On January 20,2010 President Obama delivered
his state of the union address
He sadly admitted the Democrats inherited
a financial mess
The previous administration left much to be
desired and the nations economy
quite unstable
Pres. Obama vows he won't rest without
a satisfactory solution
To this end big banks and financial wall
street must make restitution
In conclusion President Obama says cooperation
is the key if we are to lead in a
global economy
Thus the challenge that confronts the
nation must be met by you and
me

Gertrude Ayres

She was the principal of the first elementary
school I attended in Harlem
Her name was
GERTRUDE AYRES

She was the first black appointed by the city of
New York to a principality in its public school
system
Her name was
GERTRUDE AYRES

She was matronly, articulate, and greatly
respected in the academic community
Her name was
GERTRUDE AYRES

Many years have passed and the majestic image
of this black woman who raised the bar remain
within the archives of my memory
Her name was
GERTRUDE AYRES

Fun and Games

Recreation for kids in Harlem was abundant
back in the day
The city's economy was sound and programs
kept kids from going astray
Churches, public schools, and the P.A.L.
worked hard to improve the quality of life
Thus any kid with issues found a path to
truth not merely one of strife
For kids who did survive the devil in the
street, recreation was the key
It opened doors to fun and games and
no one charged a fee

The Train and The Trolley

Once upon a time, the trolley and the subway train,
before
it found a hole, ran above the ground

It contribution to the residents of Harlem was
indeed
profound

However negative aspects of these huge machines
rattled people's nerves

Lord know the noise was deafening when the steel
wheels of these monsters met those rusty
curves

Thus the days of the train and trolley inevitably
came
to pass

Sadly the demise of these friendly giants became
parts of Harlem's past

Good Ole Boys Network

I always wondered just what is the Good Ole
Boys Network

I went to Webster's dictionary and found no
Evidence that violated their worth

The Good Ole Boys seem to thrive on being non-
inclusive

When minorities attempt to join, the Good
Ole Boys even become abusive

The network likes to circulate the goodies
Among their own

Thus according to tradition, you must a be a Good
Ole Boy to even get a bone

The Dumbwaiter

Years ago, tenement houses in Harlem had within
its structure a
contraption known as a dumbwaiter

Who knows it may have been the forerunner to the
modern
elevator

The difference was it did not carry people only
discarded
trash

Therefore when loading and unloading, gloves
were required
to avoid a possible rash

When trash reached the basement, you hear the
super
yell, "I'm overloaded, don't send down no more."

On a scale of one to ten, dumbwaiters served a
purpose only
to be replaced by plastic bags at the retail store

From Top/Bottom Left to Right:
Dr. Martin Luther King Jr., Nelson Mandela,
Thurgood Marshall, Shirley Chisolm 1st Black
Congress lady

From Top/Bottom L to R:
Harriet Tubman, Marcus Garvey, Mary McLeod
Bethune, Frederick Douglass

Malcolm X

From Top/Bottom L to R: W.E.B. Dubois,
Booker T. Washington, Malcolm X, Ralph Bunche

From Top/Bottom L to R: Hank Aaron, Joe Louis,
Paul Robeson, Jackie Robinson

From Top/Bottom L to R: Emmett Till, Duke Ellington,
Maynard Jackson, 1st Black Governor Wilder, VA

From Top Ctr: Matthew Henson and Bottom L to R:
Nat King Cole, Sammy Davis Junior

President Borak Obama